ISBN-13: 978-1-948920-02-5
ISBN-10: 1948920026
for more books, visit Pski's Porch:
www.pskisporch.com

Printed in U.S.A.

OLD BLUES, NEW BLUES

By John Lambremont, Sr.

In Memory of Edward Nelson Lambremont, Jr.
1929-2017

ACKNOWLEDGEMENTS

Blues In Bisbee appeared previously in *San Pedro River Review*
In Nowhereland appeared previously in *Pure Slush Volume 14*
Day Trip To Deaville appeared previously in the *Wiser* anthology
by Truth Serum Press
Sign Said and Ditch This Summer appeared previously in *Poetry Pacific*
A Boy And His Risk appeared previously in *The Paradox Literary Magazine*
The Ultimate Interface appeared previously in *Pacific Review*
Romance In A Second Language appeared previously in the *Love Like Salt* anthology by Amy Niamh Byrne
Time After Time appeared previously in the *Tic-Toc* anthology by Kind Of A Hurricane Press
Triad Monitions appeared previously in the *Journeys Along The Silk Road* anthology by Lost Tower Publications
The Point At Montauk appeared previously in the Bards Against Hunger's fifth-year anniversary anthology
Life Without Sunglasses and Pyrites appeared previously in *Aquillrelle Wall* Number Seven
Regrets appeared previously in the *Remember* anthology by Paragram
In The Off Season appeared previously in *East Coast Literary Review*
Lefty appeared previously in *The Poeming Pigeon* Volume 21
Her Father's Daughter appeared previously in the *Tranquility* anthology by Kind Of A Hurricane Press
One From The Cajun Navy appeared previously in the *Rising Rains* anthology by Local Gems Poetry Press
Wool-O'-The-Wisp appeared previously in *The Poetry Of Flowers* anthology by Lost Tower Publications
American Dream: The Movie appeared previously in the *Truth* anthology by Truth Serum Press

Still Waiting appeared previously in the *Hope Springs A Turtle* anthology by Lost Tower Publications

To My Octogenarian appeared previously in *The Poetic Bond II*

At Mallard's Bluff appeared previously in *Flint Hills Review*

The Hope Of America appeared previously in *Cantos*

A Short Dive From The Low Board appeared previously in *Silver Birch Press*

What Is Left appeared previously in *Into The Void*

Leaf, Snake, And Butterfly appeared previously in the *Liminal Time, Liminal Spaces* anthology by Between The Lines Publishing

The Trick To Elevation appeared previously in *The Chaffin Journal*

Contents

Blues In Bisbee

Most of the musicians are grizzled veterans,
with years of riding the Southwest circuit
from Los Angeles to Lubbock and Abilene
and all the stops in between, save
the piano-pounding lady
that also wails on tenor sax
and the youthful Navajo power trio
whose blues-tinged psychedelia
a la Jimmy the Page
and Jimi the King,
wows the aging crowd.

Shade is in short supply,
and breezes are blessings,
as this heat is no longer dry,
even at a mountain altitude;
humidity is at an all-time high,
in the Rockies, Boulder is awash,
and it's cats and dogs in Albuquerque.

You find escape in a jungle gym's base,
a corner with shade and a good view of the stage,
and it's okay; most kids here are someone's grand-kids,
though they are few and far between,
and the swing and slide and monkey bars
are holding them in sway.

Bandanas out-number baseball caps,
and tattoos out-do fake boobs,
although both are in abundance.

Sixty is the new twenty-five,
as boomers and hippies that have survived
try to do their best with less
to keep their fading dreams alive.

Strats are the axes of choice,
and they take you back to the time
you let a white '64 with matching tube amp
slide right on by; the reformed rocker
who had relegated himself to the Church
was almost giving them away.
You realize now it was better that way,
your meager chops could never match
the virtuosity on display today;

then you remind yourself
that your desire to buy had been selfish once again,
the trip back then had been made for your son,
who'd admired guitars and wanted one.
You bought him a brand-new Squire instead,
but the lessons you gave him were mostly Watch Me,
so they came to an early end.
The guitar he abandoned
to a spot beneath his bed,
another example of your failure
to let him into your head,
symbolic of what came between you:
your self-imposed slight wedge.

You wonder what you can ever do
make it all up to him,
as life has no do-overs,
and you can't go back again.
Then you stare down at dry pebbles

beneath the clouding sky,
and watch as rain drops start to well up
in both your downcast eyes.

On New Years' Contrasts

This new first day is cold,
blustery, wet, and raw,
but the Laotian rose
is still in full bloom,
due to one of many
warm Christmases.

I have seen this plant in
vast numbers in Youngsville,
where lies the Lao temple
and a small Lao community.
The Lao, like the Thai,
celebrate New Year's in April;
unlike other Buddhists, who
in accordance with celestial dictates,
have their three-day observance
in February or early March.

My first trip to Lao New Years'
filled me with revelations:
a parade with floats and throws,
meat grills burning throughout temple grounds,
mass consumptions of liquor and beer,
and revelry to the point of drunkenness;
but all were happy, there was no fighting,
young and old danced together
to music screaming from a PA
in both traditional and modern styles;
vendors sold food, meats, and souvenirs;
I bought my rose that day.

I visit our Viet tam bao seldom,
where all the meat is tofu,
and where the lions' dance
and the firecracker chain
are the loudest noises of the day.

For me, this year should be
a year of change; as
my monkey Zodiac
on the Chinese calendar
has come around again,
but I have broken one resolution
and nearly broken another one
already.

By the end of this year,
through no fault of my own,
I will be a Sexagenarian.

A Tooth Is Loose

To lose a tooth
while deep in dream
is a portent of death,
my wife's people say;

but what do you do
when they crumble like chalk
and their vapid dust gathers
all over your clothes?

Perhaps the powder
can be interred,
to grow more teeth;
to sow more grief.

A Tell-Tale Fable

An old man of the old country
trods slowly over hills and dales,
his meager money in his pouch,
toward the town down in the valley
to buy supplies and a gift for his wife.

He is set upon by robbers
who beat him, rob him,
and cut wide open his throat,
so he lies still in the warm grass
to bleed out and to die.

He then sees a maiden in the distance
walking alone, a jug on her head,
her form shapely and her face attractive;
so with his last dying breaths,
he props himself up on one elbow
to watch her rotund derriere
sway in tandem with the jug,
which does not spill a drop
as she disappears over a crest.

In Nowhereland

In Nowhereland,
all the people are tan,
have dirty blonde hair,
grey dishwater eyes,
intonations that are monotonal,
and affects that are flat.

They complain there are no jobs,
but what jobs there are,
they refuse to take,
so they subsist mainly
on government subsidies
and rations in cans.

Their homes are few and far between,
pre-fabricated and shoddy,
and their yards large enough to be plots,
ill-defined but not disputed,
but the landscaping is spotty.

The government sends out initiatives,
often on home beautification,
but without sufficient incentive,
and in the sway of sweltering heat,
the Nowherelanders' attempts
at compliance are half-hearted,
and the results sporadic.

Their population is thinning,
so the authorities urge procreation,

but they find fornication a chore,
and prefer to lie about
on their chosen indoor spots;
orality is the norm,
and offends no one's morality,
as long as it's not too hot.

Day Trip To Deaville

If you ever have to cross
the state line to go to Deaville,
there are a few things
you should know before you go.

The town is both the creation
and the victim of
the polymer plastics plant
and boosted and betrayed it;
the decayed art-deco architecture
of the old townhouses and downtown
reflect its past swells in population,
but few live there anymore;
the plant was shut down by the E.P.A.,
and all but the poor and afflicted
have long since moved away.

Dr. DeMerritt is a kindly old soul,
and he fits his poisoned patients,
limp limbs ground down to stumps,
with prostheses fashioned
from the same synthetic,
blast-heated to inert form,
that poured for years through leaky valves
and broken pipes, and leached
into the groundwater below;
but the clinic shares a building
with the jail; be careful
what door you enter
and let close behind you;

you might have a hard time
talking your way out.

When it is time to leave,
turn right and right and right again,
as that is the only way out of town;
a left turn anywhere will lead
to a series of Do Not Enters
and Dead Ends, and you will
end up right back where
you started from again;

and whatever you do,
never enter the tunnel;
it is inhabited by subterraneans
that for varying sham reasons
never got even a small share
of the class action settlement;
they are unruly beyond resentment,
and will gladly stop your car
and molest you, or worse.

Cloud

From behind her turned shoulder
her face cannot be seen: she sits,
spent and folded, the weight
of the heavens on her back.
Her gown is solid gray, her hair
tousled clumps of white wisp.
She holds her head in her hands,
her elbows on bent knees,
for she is grief replete in loss
of a loved son, her day gone,
her sky now dark and fallen.

A Boy And His Risk

A boy sits in the back
of his mother's car. He finds
what looks to be a peach pit
or some kind of nut.
He is wary, as he
has heard or been told
that the inner parts of peach pits
are poisonous, deadly so.

He starts to fiddle with
the orb's wrinkled husk;
its skin crumbles beneath
his fingers, but the shell
resists. He worries at
the gnarled surface
with his tips and nails.
The work is slow,
and done out of eye.
After a long while,
a little hole is made,
and the shell pried apart.

A small brown kernel
is revealed. He takes
it, eyes it, sniffs it.
He considers briefly
his consequences,
then puts the seed
into his mouth and
crunches it. The taste

that results is so
delicious that he
doesn't care if his folly
does him in.

A Baseball Life

A muddy, old baseball
is left by the curb,
stuck deep in a puddle,
cheers no longer heard,
neglected by all
for the wear it incurred.

The life of a baseball
is long, hard, and rough;
it's valued by all
when it's without a scuff,
then it bounces off walls
and rolls through grass and dust.

Soon past its prime,
the ball's put in a bag,
and time after time,
it is pitched, hit, and shagged
until the seams unwind
and its skin's in sag;

and then its life's over,
the ball becomes waste,
buried in clover,
a foul gone astray,
or hit by a mower,
or just thrown away.

Dirge Day

Another cold Thursday rain;
four dark birds over wires
mark black notes
in a gray chart
of mourning refrain.

In internal pianos,
broken and out-of-tune,
hammers clunk clumsily
a worn and weary patter
on deadened strings.

Gather we in masses,
stalled in rites of passage;
we breathe collected gasses,
the price at the pumps
not so dear as the death
that draws us closer;

and the weariest movements
of our winter symphony,
frozen coda and icy finale,
as yet are nowhere near;
storms we will later hear
form still in the baton
of the Conductor.

No End To Suffering

Three caskets on a knoll.
Three names picked at random.
Three robed monks preside.

Three souls to be interred alive,
to meditate and wait
for Death to arrive.

The first is infirm,
the second elderly;
I am the third.

I don't understand
how I can be chosen;
I am but a guest;

still, I feel obliged.

The chanting of the faithful
is plaintive and melancholic,
wood blocks are sounded, bell bowls rung.

With one final chorus,
the prelude is over,
the end has begun.

At the very last moment,
I turn aside; I cannot fulfill
my duty to die.

The senior monk tells me
that I am excused; and as a non-believer,
I will not be blamed.

An elder woman
at the end of her days
volunteers to take my place;

still, I feel ashamed.

Ciudad Victoria

The two young wayfarers
on their way to Puebla
leave Monterrey early
on a New Year's Day,
resolution determination
to go all the way
until they reach their destination;

and as they drive southward,
the terrain gently changes,
from flat scrub and cactus
to grassy gold pastures,
then rolling pine hills
that incline toward the mountains.

At a hill-side road tavern
where they stop for a beer,
the younger surrenders
his prized cowboy hat
to a smiling gang chieftain
that likes its construction;
they vow *no mas cervezas*
'til this time the next day;

then they soon discover
the treasure of the Sierras
is the bountiful orchards
grown on rowed hills and mountains;
all attended in road stands
by young sons of the owners;

juices squeezed fresh and poured cheap,
so they drink their fill.

At the edge of Victoria,
they stare down the green river,
amazed at the verdance
of the tropical forest,
and the parrots and monkeys
that dot the lush foliage.

In the city's main *zócalo*
there's a wedding reception;
they pause at the iron gates, looking inside;
then they are invited
to come in and imbibe,
but they are steered away
from the maids of the bride.

They take a late supper
at a small hotel's restaurant;
its jovial owner
implores them to stay:
the road through the mountains
es muy peligroso,
and many have frozen
once wrecked on the way;

but they sense a sales pitch,
and decline the offer;
they'll reach the Great City
by morning this way,
then on to Puebla
by the middle of day;

so they mount the Toyota,
and head up the highway,
straight toward the mountains
so darkened at night;
and they cannot see yet
the hell that awaits them,
a rough night of sleeplessness,
terror, and fright.

Today At Karfas Bay

We sit on the bow
of a small beached boat;
it has not seen the sea
for some time.

The hills and mounts of Turkey,
eight miles across blue water,
have never seemed as close
than on this pristine day.

Brown sea peat seaweed,
as thick as primordial muck,
blankets the sands in mounds,
as if it had once borne
the first amphibians.

The people here are unabashed
when it comes to their bodies;
men bear their hairy bellies proudly,
and even the middle-aged women
wear two-pieces or bikinis.
Several of the smallest kids
bathe completely in the buff.

The orange café tabby cat
peers at me with old eyes.
Too sick to chew the shrimp shells tossed,
and never to reach full growth,
it will likely die later this summer,
but I give it a piece of dogfish.
Its healthier calico companion purrs,
reposed and sated at my feet.

Sign Said

For the preservation of the lucence
of the ochre in the moths
resting patently in the luxury
of the lacquer of the parlor,
please refrain from lighting
pipes, cigars, or cigarettes
past the arbor near the door
that opens to the foyer.
Thanks for helping,
signed, the Owners.

What Happened To Donald

His condos on the river rocks
were starting to fall apart,
and quickly filled with trash.

His digs in The Caverns
contained a comfy bed,
but the path to the bath
went right through his room,
and there was no view.

The fortune-telling pianist
went from chair to chair,
but when she got to Donald,
she frowned and moved on.

His street and dam construction
bogged down in mid-stream,
leaving us no access
to his casino boat.

The denouements and closings
of his last correspondences
were incomprehensible gibberish,
and looked more like Farsi.

His last shot fell through;
the net crumbled and broke off,
and the ball was nearly flat.

Waiting For The Dog To Poo

In the lull between storms,
the wind in the pines
is an ominous reminder
of what I have done
and have yet to do.

Accomplishments are swept aside,
past failures readily remembered;
my life is a series of conflicts
from which I do not flinch,
but they leave me tired;
my mind is a sieve
through which thoughts
pour through too easily;
and despite plethoric emotions,
I struggle mightily
with words.

A Course With No Name

What was once to be
the golf and tennis resort
and retirement community
was abandoned half-completed,
the developer but one casualty
of the killer hurricane
and accompanying tornadoes,
and when the levees failed again,
the entire project went under,
awash with tide and swamp waters,
and no pumping station
within twenty miles;

but the unfinished houses and structures
were soon inhabited by a strange
mix of squatters: migrant Latinos,
swampers, rowdy rednecks,
fur trappers, and coloureds
of every color fled the city.
They made homes in ravaged frames
with ramshackle ingenuity,
and soon bateaus and pirogues
could be found in most driveways.

We went there in curiosity,
having seen the feature on T.V.,
and we were surprised when
the bearded guy in the pro shop
said we could play the course for free,
but when we asked for a cart,
he just sneered.

The fairways were overgrown meadows
merged with the surrounding forests,
and hardly playable for the downed trees,
with standing water everywhere,
but the greens were even worse;
someone had decided to drain them
through holes at the lowest spots,
so every putt rolled like a gum-
ball through a vending machine,
around the rim and slowly down,
falling ultimately into the cup,
so we quit after two holes.

Out by the club-house,
through the application
of orange highway barrels,
huge sheets of visqueen,
and copious amounts of chlorine,
some semblance of a pool remained,
and dozens of kids in floaties
or clutching foam noodles
bobbed around in blue-green water,
all as happy as clams.

The Fatalist Arises

Let the early morning sun
shine through the open window
and soothe my fluttering guts;

as save the simple ascetic,
we are all addicted to food:
each of us must have it
each and every day;

thus, do not spoil the food
with fingers that waggle,
heads that shake, or
tongues that cluck;
let each have his own.

In The Court Of The Sanguine King

The Accuser has barricaded himself
in his wine cellar, where he dabs
at the scratches on his face,
harangues the Accused via intercom
as to the whereabouts of his wife,
and warns him that his house
has been secured from the outside,
and the authorities are on their way.

The Accused has turned the tables
by hanging himself by his feet
from the top of the parlor ceiling
and pouring all of his blood out
onto the tile floor below,
using the Accuser's straight razor
as the means of arterial entry.

The Petit Jurors file into the parlor,
each letting out a gasp or grunt
as they survey the grisly scene,
and form a seated semi-circle.

The Judge Examiner is late, as usual,
and harrumphs as he enters the room.
One thing, he says, he is sure of already:
The Fly Man is near to dying.

The Fly Man, faded to a chalky
black-and-white, is flustered
by the Judge's presumption,

but acknowledges the impending end
of his earthly existence.

The Accuser is brought forward,
and his face blanches visibly
at the state of the Accused
and the order of the Judge
for samples of tissues.

The wife is never found.

I Am Not Dead

I am so deep in the doghouse,
I take my solitary refuge
down at the old school-yard,
flattened cardboard boxes my bed,
and a ragged sheet my cover;

but still, I cannot sleep,
my hips thrust and twitch
in contorted convulsions
of frustrated impotency.

I find myself speed-sleeping,
dreaming that I am awake,
and conscious of so being;
my heart-beats slow to nothing,
and I am barely breathing;
I cannot move a muscle.

Professor Louviere hovers over me now,
conducting a visual examination,
and makes his field notations
into a hand-held recording device.
All of his murmured observations
are based on one flawed premise.

The Ultimate Interface

All the private sector
was shut down for a day,
so that all the working people
could stay home and participate,
and the stores and malls were closed.

Multi-outlets were set up
in parks and public places,
so that those without
the requisite technology
would not be disenfranchised.

Through the intricacies of programming
and the new generation of eyeglass screens,
the people could watch, pretty much,
anything they wanted, whether sports,
movies, theater, dance, opera, history,
news, network, reality, re-runs,
documentaries, talk, music videos,
or even non-pornographic love-making,
and all could view up to sixteen
channels simultaneously.

The proffered reason was
a well-earned day of leisure,
but you had better believe
that every viewer was recorded,
and subversives and intellectuals noted.

The Universal Ass-Clown

What comes next
you have seen before,
somewhere,
in some form,
at some time.

You stand downtown in wait for a parade.
Near you, in a walled driveway,
a gathering of young adults,
apparently family and friends,
have created a clan-cave
against the rear steel door,
lawn chairs and ice chests
their furniture, a small barbecue pit
their source of heat and food.

They could be from Anywhere,
an average-looking bunch,
mid-twenties to late-thirties,
casually dressed and properly festooned,
hot dogs in one hand,
beers or cocktails in the other,
veggies, chips, and dips at the ready
for grazing.

The males of this tribe
emit as announcement or greeting
long howls of manly delight,
"Wooooooooooooooooooooooooo!"
boisterous but annoying,
but, hey, it's a holiday.

From up the block, you hear
the calls of an elder member.
You can tell by his glazed expression,
a hideous frozen bake-lite smile,
that he is far past toast
and way beyond caring.

He stumbles into their cluster,
howling his greeting to every male member,
and within a few minutes,
all three of his sheets to the wind
have sagged and collapsed.
Three of his throng provide cover
while he pees leaning on a wall,
then he fights a losing battle with gravity,
nearly falling as he clings to a utility box post.
He is led finally to a lawn chair,
where he sits, whipped, and equipped
with a plastic bag atop his paunch
and a cup of water in the arm holster.

The parade has finally started,
and you try to enjoy it,
but you can't stop your head
from turning to see what's next.
The drunk is spitting up into his bag
and nearly choking on his sippy cup.
His bag is exchanged, and two
of the females wipe his face
with several wet paper towels.
Later, you see he has passed out,
the strain gone from his moon face,
and his peaceful and cherubic countenance
prompts his nursies to decorate him,
their brave stalwart.

It starts with a frisbee ring thrown
from a float, which makes a tidy halo;
next, two foam mini soccer balls
to augment his moobs.
They decide the best use for him
is as a bead receptacle, and proceed
to adorn him accordingly.
One of his two ladies fair pauses
twice to puke neatly
into a sidewalk storm drain,
going back immediately to imbibe more
of whatever it was she was drinking;
a real gamer, her.

Soon the whole tribe catches on,
forms a semi-circle around
their sleeping arch-duke, and clamors
to the floats for their attention.
The gents riding up top survey
the situation, and unleash a surplus
of their biggest beads, competing
in range and accuracy.
Many hit the prostrate valiant,
the rest are gathered and draped
properly by the tribe.
Soon, the sodden day-warrior
resembles the jeweled center-piece
of a pharaoh's extravagant funeral, covered
with hundreds of strings of shining beads,
their multi-colors glittering
in the mid-day sun.
The fallen leader comes to
occasionally, tries to smile,
and succumbs once more.

You are still gawking,
and your head and neck are
thwacked by some large beads thrown,
which hurt like hell.
Serves you right, you say
to yourself, and you tell your wife
you are ready to leave,
as the parade is nearly over,
and the float her kinfolks rode on
has already passed. She agrees,
so you turn away abruptly
without a look back.

In the end, you are disgruntled,
and in silent contemplation,
you just have to wonder
why God ever bothered
with man's creation
In the Beginning.

Oh, Well

No one was sure
if it was bought in a store
or raised for such a purpose.

It was left at the door
in a basket with a bow,
but there was no note found.

It failed to perform
as hoped and expected,
and was thus set aside,
left unattended,
and so it died.

Such is life
down on The Farm;
work is hard,
and death is
always around.

The Alien

Jet fighter pilots wear masks,
and astronauts do, too.
I once saw a fighter pilot's mask
disintegrate from contamination
from a space-borne microbe,
but that was in a movie.

Now I wear a mask nightly.
It helps me get more air
into my lungs because
my heart and brain need oxygen
that I can't give them.

It helps me sleep better, too,
and I am no longer fatigued
in the early afternoon,
but my deeper slumbers
cause me to lose my dreams,
and my wife calls me The Alien.

My son tells me all about
the symptoms of my affliction,
even though I relate that
I've read about them already.
He asks me if I want to die in my sleep.
I say yes.

Une Ode De L'Odeur

You can kidnap me,
blindfold me,
take me away
for a number of days
to a far distant land,
but if you return me
to one certain place,
with my bound, sightless face,
I'll still know where I stand.

Better shove plugs
in my squinting ears, too,
as the sounds of this street
would too soon tell the tale,
but the best give-away
to this mystery and veil
is the smell, night and day,
that would turn the dead pale.

Inside your nostrils,
a fingerprint scent,
a strong and indelible
stirred cesspool mess
of horse feed and hayseeds,
mule stools and piss,
hair spray and hair pomade,
milk soured thick, sewer lines,
patchouli, bags of refuse,
bikers' pipes, beer, sweat,
and cheap, sweet perfume,

sticky red puddles
of hurricane puke; and
you won't smell the Bourbon,
but it's there for you.

The Manliest Man

I was suspicious of the show
from the very beginning;
the cable network was obscure
and not even on my grid,
the sets were second-hand,
the equipment out-of-date;
the host was a nobody,
the crew was indifferent,
and there were no scenic locales.

Nonetheless, I entered the tryouts,
and much to my uneasy surprise,
I was named one of three finalists;
the other two were an aging cowboy
and an inflated former body-builder:
I guess I represented Mr. Average.

The contest was not about
exceptional feats of courage
or strength; rather, we were placed
into semi-ordinary situations and measured
as to the appropriateness of our responses
under today's standards of manliness.

One such endeavor involved donning
a woman's skirt and blouse and trying to explain
the reason why to your father.
There was no live feed for him to see;
they e-mailed him still pictures, and called
on the telephone for his reaction,

with a photo of him circa 1988
posted on the monitor's screen.
I told him that the get-up
was for a theme-based party,
not for a life-style change,
and he said he was relieved.

In another test of manliness,
we were instructed assume
a bad humor and walk up
a crowded studio sidewalk,
where aggressive persons
tried to bump into us.
This time, I could hear
the instructions clearly
and finally got to go last.
The cowboy muttered angrily,
and the body builder threatened
to whip somebody's ass,
so when my time came,
I pivoted nimbly away from collisions,
saying "Excuse me" at each turn.
I explained to the producers
that when I am truly mad
I shun contact with strangers,
but I don't think they bought it.

A third challenge was presented
by an unruly five year old child.
I knew from sad life experience
that yelling, threats, and spankings
usually did little if any good,
so I bribed the tyke with ice cream.

I never found out if I was cutting
the mustard, or was on the right track;
the project was shelved, suddenly
and permanently, pre-pilot,
never to be revived again.

Toad Under Toe

A strange sensation most grotesque,
immediate in recognition,
never forgotten once
encountered:

a squalid, clammy legged bag
of bloated protoplasm
bearing small bones thrashing
in sweating desperation.

Uncertain of the damage done,
the ball longs to roll forward
to dispatch; the toe shudders
and wants to withdraw.

Per the past proclamations of a Rooster,
there are only two things to know:
either kill it or let it go.

Sometimes the toad wears fine clothes.
Sometimes the toe bears fine hose.

Trust

Trust is a troublesome concept;
it requires more than hope or faith,
it assumes a certain understanding,
and as everyone says or seems to know,
assume makes an ass of "u" and "me."

Trust is a tricky word;
it contains elements of truth
that form the basis of a truce,
but without the first T,
it turns to rust,
without the last T,
it resembles a truss,
a form of support
in some ways like the trust
that can bolster sagging hope
or raise up lagging faith,
but always at the core of trust
is "us."

Trust is like money;
it can be lent, spent,
withheld or withdrawn,
invested, expended,
but in the end,
trust is only as worthy
as the person or Concept
in receipt of its extension.

Another Gray Day

Back in the car again, silver sky in wilt,
Don Drummond is still in session,
just as he was last night,
backed by the other Skatalites,
and conducted by Sir Coxsone.

The tunes are sunny but ominous,
products of unrest that do not reveal
themselves, as dark as the heart
of Jamaica itself, a reminder
of life's grit and bumpiness;
yet, they, like we, chug along,
our little motors humming
as we try to do our best,
in wait for the next cold front:
plus ça change, plus c'est
la même chose.

Our son has come down for the holidays,
and has since come down with a head cold,
but tonight will find him a new venue,
La Maison La Coeur, where he will partake
of paté, sweetbreads, and the chocolate heart,
to add an *accent aigu* to a winter still
in start.

The Griever

The blue lieutenant
in search of his lost wife
asked the mountain's gate-keeper
for the origin of the tributary,
adding that was likely where
we would find his body.

We course upstream
on the cliff's stone face
and pluck the left eye
of the first dead president;
inside they lie entwined near
the pond that formed the stream,
tear ducts of eternity.

Romance In A Second Language

The café is crowded, and the crowd
is too boisterous; loud voices,
hearty laughs, and flirty giggles
fill her eardrums like the screech
of a hundred locusts.

His face is earnest in address,
furtive as he glances aside,
his mumbling kept low,
and only the simplest words are caught
in her net of comprehension.

Tiny icebergs afloat in her martini show
that nothing is straight up here;
she cannot discern whether
this is the end of a brief encounter
or the beginning of a great adventure.

Her solitary tear plops into her drink,
sending ripples across the crystal,
a little extra saltiness in the glass
sea of Bombay, as what was once buoyant
is now slowly deflating.

He grasps her wrist limply
to take her pulse.

De Minimus

Siding, remorse,
storm doors,
and garden hose.

Communicate via
tiny hand signals.

Only a mother
can call him
a little boy.

The hint of a replay
turned out to be
a false alarm.

Receive the Nipper alert;
the mammals will not go lightly.

The Acid Mirror

When you first see it,
you will not believe
your eyes, as it will play
tricks on its subjects.

You may watch your face melt
as if it were hot wax, or see
your thin skull through your skin.
You may hold your hand up
to observe the green blood cells
coursing through your veins.
This is just the start.

In the corners, visions will appear
in accordance with your upbringing:
you may see Adam and Eve,
seraphim, saints, or Satan.
You may glimpse passed loved ones,
or watch yourself being born.
Do not be alarmed; these images
are coming from your brain and
its chemically-rewired synapses.
If you turn away now, you will relate
it all to a bad experience.

The acid mirror will speak to you;
it will tell you lies.
It will tell you that you can fly,
that you are invincible, immortal.
Do not listen to its whispering,

as you may end up stuck in a wall
or even much worse, like flying
in free fall;

but if you can keep yourself steady,
the acid mirror will take you seriously.
Then all of your pretensions and illusions,
your prides and prejudices,
your lies and delusions,
will be stripped away,

and what is left behind is you,
naked, unfiltered, and unadulterated,
the you from which you cannot hide.
If you are not prepared for this,
you will bum and will curl yourself
into a crying ball, so don't take
this stuff lightly;

but if you can face the truth,
lean into the acid mirror so closely
that your dilated pupils become
mirrors to the mirror.
In them you will see multiple
and telescoping imprints of yourself,
calm, smiling, and extending
into Infinity.

Farewell

After the final blessings,
the multi-colored balloons,
now children of the sky,
all the same shape and size,
released at the same time,
leave the procession behind
to rise slowly toward the tree-line.

A measure of God's breath
lifts them over the live oaks;
not a single string snags.
They hold close in a cluster
to ascend and to recede,
from spots to dots to specks,
then disappear completely
into white clouds on high.

Time After Time

Brubeck made time Rubikal,
the permutations never-ending,
transitions seamless,
a custom cruise bike
rolling down a hill
to a coast around a new lake,
but parked in a familiar place
always.

Bird contracted time,
squeezed more from himself
than any before or since,
and time contracted him,
the beautiful blue odonata
beating his lace wings to pieces
on the burning light bulb.

Monk turned time on its ear
and made it space,
the fox in the barnyard
that called out the tunes,
and all the animals
danced the wiggly.

Billie made time slow down
and take a longer look,
her languorous reticent flirtation
an allure of expression,
making time instantly
immortal;

and Louie,
dear Louie, sweet Louis,
with one strong arm made
time stand still.

Beware

It may appear as a black box
sitting on a road shoulder
that teases your periphery
as you drive by.

It may be a crack
in a side-walk, a gap
between buildings,
or a hole in a cloud.

Do not slow down to look.
Do not pause, and
whatever you do,
do not linger.

These are apertures
of the universe;
they will suck you in
and take you away,
if you let them.

If you are not careful,
you will be transported
in space or time
to God knows where,
perhaps a jaunty past
of lagoons and harpoons;
perhaps to a non-existence
of perpetual doom.

You will someday fall prey
to one of these seams;
it is something we all do.

From Two Scientists, One

In the background,
her siblings frolic in the surf
of a summer sea.

In the foreground,
on a broad expanse of sugar beach,
a nearly newly-born human being lies
on her back on her father's surfboard,
her head turned away from an overcast sun,
her ruffled hat adjusted to protect her face.
Her fists are curled tight to her chest,
and her feet lift slightly and kick,
but her movement is her dark eyes;
they roam and search incessantly
to try to connote her own cosmos,
the inquisitive but not yet focused peering
of a future naturalist or astronomer.

Her eyes lock in briefly
on the lens.
Click.

At The Overlook

The fat man climbs,
as dainty as a ballerina,
Rolleiflex and lenses in hand,
over the rail to trod
onto a rock outcropping
for post-card quality panoramas.
His wife calls out her concern.
Those more acrophobic
join hands, trudge slowly
to the edge, peer down,
and retreat, shaking
their heads.

The Canyon is a mountain
upside-down, its ridge
a green snake that coils
and slithers under a sun
that lights but provides little
heat. A man descending will
lose his life here today,
another statistic, yet
barely newsworthy;

but no body can deny
the vast and scenic majesty
of the great ancient crevasse,
encompassing the unwary eye
as far as it can see;
boulders, brush, and sage
provide an earthen pallet

for rams and jackrabbits to play
beneath a blue eternity.

The sight of a giant horseshoe,
glass-bottomed and extending,
brings at least one viewer,
fearful and trembling internally,
to his figurative knees.

Devoid

On this cold eve,
stars do not sparkle, but
glitter queerly in the face
of Blue Night, zirconic pasties
and bits of broken glass
scattered then fixed,
yet spreading still
in futile sterility,
leaving us barren.

Separation becomes loss,
disappointment catastrophe,
distance widens within
tired familiar spaces;
we catch the drift,
the loss of nearness,
constellations of contrast
that spin slowly apart,
inexorable in regression,
and weary of company.

At times like this,
we are old ghosts
who haunt the lives
of each other.

By My Reckoning

No one wants
to be a statistic,
but every one of us
is one.

In modern societies,
there are entire statistical
categories about how
many statistical
categories to which
each of us
belongs.

Even the smallest tribe of pygmies,
or the wildest band of aborigines,
living unknown in the world
in an undiscovered corner,
are made to be statistics
by the educated guesses
of learned men
in universities,
but also keep
their own numbers
on their own;

while the guru atop the mountain,
living alone, remote and aloof,
finds he is his sole company,
and so makes a statistic
of himself, albeit
unwittingly.

The Once-Tender Widow

He first met the English lieutenant
in the second year of the war;
the young officer was assigned
as the attaché to their company,
newly-arrived from the States.
They had mutual tastes in music,
and soon became fast friends,
hiking the hills together in off hours
while the lieutenant, already
an accomplished crooner,
sang popular songs of the day,
and the Yank comped on guitar.
Then, unfortunately, as it came to pass,
they had eyes for the same woman.

She was the lovely Lady Bailes,
a widow whose flyer husband
was shot down over the Channel
early in the Battle of Britain.
After a suitable mourning period,
she accepted certain male callers,
among them the two friends.
She was warm to the American,
but her face would light up visibly
when her countryman came around;
yet, the Englishman feigned ambivalence
despite his growing affection,
and the American kept a secret,
in deference to his friendship,
of his helpless love and infatuation.

After their respective forays across Europe,
they returned to London to find
that their lady fair had fallen
on hard times. Her husband's estate
was largely his home, effects, and title;
what money he'd left was long gone,
and with no family, his or hers, to help her,
she had cut off her long black locks,
dyed her hair bright platinum blonde,
and had taken to whoring.
The Englishman, freshly mustered from the service,
and finding success as a popular singer,
found her situation ironic and amusing,
and did not hesitate to visit with his friends,
sometimes for all-night group revelries,
but still he could not hide a strange jealousy
that no one could understand.

The American, aghast and distressed,
mostly stayed away from the awful scenario,
but his love for the widow did not diminish.
Soon to be sent back Stateside, he tried
to figure a way to save the Lady from her plight,
and finally concocted a grand plan:
he would marry the widow in a secret ceremony,
then take her back to his home town,
where nobody knew of her past,
and they could start a new life together.

After pacing alone the next afternoon.
he went that evening to profess his love,
and to extend his proposition of marriage,
but found her house dark and foreboding,
and his door-bell ring went unanswered.

He went around to the side door,
and found it unlocked and slightly ajar,
so he slipped into the unlit kitchen.
From upstairs he heard low music,
so he crept up the stairs slowly,
and peered into the master bedroom.
There he found the Lady Bailes lying
dead on the floor in a pool of fresh red blood,
her husband's prized saber protruding
from a stab wound deep in her breast.

He bit his fist in shock and anguish,
then gingerly pulled the saber from her,
laying it carefully at her side.
Not knowing what else to do,
he picked up the telephone
and called the authorities
to report the violent crime.

He was then arrested and indicted,
as his finger-prints were on the murder weapon,
his call came in within minutes of her death,
and he had no one to verify his whereabouts.
He was put on trial for manslaughter,
as his was a crime of passion, after all,
and the case was followed closely by the tabloids.
In accordance with popular sentiment,
he was convicted in a unanimous verdict,
and sentenced to a gaol term of fifteen years.

After serving a twelve-year stretch,
he was released for good behavior,
and placed in house arrest awaiting deportation.
He learned that the Bailes home had been purchased

by his former English army friend and comrade,
now a world-famous star of screen and stage,
where he had taken up residency when in town.
The American, risking the terms of his probation,
snuck out one night to take a look at the house,
and found himself again standing before the side door.
Finding it unlocked, he opened it slowly,
and slipped through the kitchen into the parlour.

Once there, he was astonished to find
that the Englishman had turned the house
into some type of macabre museum:
on darkened walls illuminated by spotlights
were a near-dozen blown-up photographs,
taken from happier times and occasions,
of the once-tender widow, of himself
and his former colleague, and of the three
of them together, all of their faces smiling
and turned toward their photographers.
On a table he found newspapers and tabloids
covering the Lady's passing and his trial,
and a small but expensive tape-recorder.
Set to low volume, he turned the device on,
and listened in complete and utter amazement
to a discussion between top British officials
on how to pin the Bailes case on him;
it would be a shame, they said, to tarnish
the name of the bright, rising singing star,
decorated in service to Her Majesty,
and quite bad for the struggling public morale,
so the American would be made a ready scape-goat,
and would face a lesser charge to reduce
whatever ancillary damage might be done.
He stopped the tape and stood silently

to gather his thoughts and his wits.
He saw on the coffee table two empty bottles
of the finest imported French cognac
and next to them a half-full china cup;
draped over the sofa was a silk smoking jacket
with a monogram of his former friend's initials
embroidered in gold thread on the left breast.
He then heard deep snoring coming
from a second floor bedroom above.
Mounted over the fireside mantle,
he found hanging the tell-tale saber,
and he took it down reflectively,
gripping it with both hands grimly
as he headed toward the stair-well
in resolute and final determination
to complete the grisly circle.

His stay in prison this time around
was just more than twenty-two years;
he had violated his probation, after all,
and had murdered a famous performer
much celebrated at home and abroad.
Once released, he was removed quickly,
and sent back to his native America
to live out what was left of his life.

He settled in The Quarter in New Orleans,
never once thinking of taking a wife,
where he lived quietly and modestly
in a ground-floor minute apartment,
busking in the streets in the day-time
and playing gigs in the small bars by night.
In one such dark and smoky venue,
I made his acquaintance two summers ago.

After introductory chat and several high-balls,
he told me this story, real and complete,
and gave me his true permission
to write this poem and print it.

Regime Change

What I found incredible
was not the rapidity with
which the reigning ruler
lost the realm, but
rather the fact that
his ninth daughter lived
in an apartment where
all the door locks,
latches, and throws
were dysfunctional; so,

when the baby-blue
and white-clad cadre
of rebel troops cased
the building, they easily
found me hiding in
a back bedroom
behind a screen.
Their lieutenant exclaimed
that as an obvious C.I.A.
operative, I would be
an asset to the new regime,
but only after months
of re-education
and conditioning; thus,

after being suitably
suited, booted, and hatted,
I was paraded up the
grand boulevard toward

the presidential palace, proclaimed
as a prime example
of how the revolution
was truly multi-cultural.

The Two-Hundred Pound Annoyance

To bring him again to the temple spring festival
seems to be a sad mistake repeated:
he spends little time with the family,
picks at their vegetarian fare, and doesn't care
for the traditional singing and dancing.
Instead, he walks the grounds all afternoon,
plays like a child with groups of small children,
takes pictures of babies with his plastic drug-store camera,
chats with the monks, mispronouncing what words
he knows in their language, and makes awkward bows
to elders of no standing, often leaving
the property to smoke a cigarette or Whatever.

At sundown, he misses the essential procession,
and when a major downpour washes out the featured singer,
they decide to leave, but he is still AWOL.
They find him in the temple, half-soaked,
a sleeping child clinging to his neck,
her face buried in his shoulder.
Her mother sits next to him,
a silly woman who chose unwisely
to bring her five kids to the temple alone,
leaving her not enough arms
to lend any comfort to the middle child
sitting on the sidewalk and bawling
in howls of tearful outrage.

Rose In Early Bloom

She stands and sways
in a tender wind,
her stems slender
but already supple,
her lips pursed,
beginning to part,
but not yet revealing
the stamen and pistils
concealed inside.

Soon she will be taken
and fit to fine trim,
her tiny thorns shorn,
she will be placed
and arranged to adorn,
along with her sisters,
a revered crystal vase
on the dining room table.

There they are family,
beneath the chandelier,
and they open up freely
to whisper of love,
to mature and ripen,
and to gossip of husbands
that will never come;

and while she will die
a withered old maid,
the image of her dancing

in the open garden air,
young and so confident,
drawing eyes from everywhere,
shall forever remain.

Triad Monitions

Take care in the disposition
of your broken-off hair:
if a bird finds one,
and weaves it into its nest,
the rest will fall out.

A turtle in your yard
is the best type of luck;
to tease or hurt it risks
an horrific twist of fate.
Give it good passage,
and see it safely
on its way.

Give thanks, and ask forgiveness
of all that you must kill,
whether a stalk or leaf to be sliced,
a fish you may take from the lake,
a red hen whose neck needs to be wrung,
or whatever it is you have to butcher;
for there is a reason why
a condemned frog crosses
his supplicant front legs
in the last moments before
the cleaver falls.

Berlin

Where even the taxis
are Audis, Benzes, and Beemers.

Where cars, bikes, and cycles are everywhere,
but there are few traffic accidents,
as all obey the rules.

Where sophisticated women,
Germanic, Nordic, and ethnic,
stroll the Torstrasse in boots,
smoking cigarettes.

Where international cuisine abounds,
but the local fare is better.

Where bottled beer is cheaper
than bottled water,
and the afternoon *späti* beer,
drunk en route on sidewalk or subway,
seems to be the norm.

Where the wursts are the best,
except for the curry-wurst,
which is the worst.

Where the only golfers on the course in carts
are us.

Where squares of brass inlaid
before the stoops of certain buildings

mark the homes of Holocaust victims,
and note their names.

Where the closely-imbedded poles
that once held up the Wall
speak in louder volumes
than the plaques and memorials surrounding.

Where my son writes at home
in humble semi-obscurity,
helpless in love again,
and hoping for acceptance.

The Waiting Game

Blackbirds gather to chatter incessantly
in the top of a tree
behind a sick man's house,
unaffected by prevailing winds.

A calico cat sits
patiently by a side door.

The man cannot greet his guests;
his Phenergan has rendered him drowsy,
so he dozes alone
in his room.

Out on the sound, sea hawks
and saints are getting chippy,
and have to be separated
on several close occasions.

The man's spotted dog,
sequestered in her kennel,
senses coming trouble,
and quietly whines
to herself.

The Point At Montauk

The striped lighthouse is an exclamation,
a stanchion bastion against the surging sea beyond,
but the fathers that founded it knew all too well
that the pounding ocean is a prodigious foe,
a relentless and unceasing batterer
of batture and all that lies below,
so they built the lighthouse high and away,
some three fields back from the rocky sands
that formed the craggy, scraggly beach.

Time has proven the founders' prescience,
as the waves' unending wear and tear
over decades and scores of two centuries plus
have worn the flinty soil away,
yard by yard and acre by acre,
imperiling the lighthouse, now a landmark,
and endangering its mission of mariners' mercy.
The solution reached was Herculean in scope,
the selection, sculpture, and careful placement
of giant slabs of black basalt and mica-flecked granite,
rising in tiers from the sea bed thirty feet upward,
forming a rip-rap of the greatest order possible,
huge building blocks laid with pyramidic precision
so as to create a make-shift walkway,
a parapet for appraisal of what next the sea might bring.

Today, Neptune's children seem playful,
gently tossing wavelets across the breach,
while two wet-suited surfers out of season
send out hoots of illicit delight
as they catch and ride briefly
the eighths of waves.

The Walking Contradiction

It is in the very nature of man
to proclaim his desire and need
for happiness, enlightenment, or salvation
in his many waking spoken words,
but not in his deeds in between.

He will argue in discourse with his fellows,
read great books without understanding,
travel great distances for new insights,
ignore his body for the sake of his mind,
live in dreams but dismiss their night messages,
and spurn those around him in scorn and abuse;

but the one thing he always refuses to do:
look down the bridge of his upturned nose,
see the path to his goal on the plain
ground before him, and move.

Better

Better use the wire brush
before the judges come,
for they award the cups
and all the ribbons.

Better drive it straight away
and keep it down the middle,
for the ditches
on both sides
are filled with water.

Better sing a soulful song
that's sweet to all the sisters,
for it's they, and they alone,
that call the tunes.

Better shake the tender hand
of the waiting good Lord Jesus,
for you know your time
is coming, and it's soon.

Life Without Sunglasses

The tiny arachnid, having gathered herself
on the broad expanse of hotel pillow,
never sees the approach of the globe
that crushes her, only a shadow on the case,
large and looming, which prompts
her instinctive reaction, a tensing
in ready of defense, her mouth agape,
and when the guest's head hits,
she bites the flesh before her,
injects a web of venom
into a fluttering eyelid,
and in a last desperate act
of preservation intended,
tries vainly to secrete her eggs.

The guest is an average specimen
of the variety *Oafus Learned*,
and feels a slight eye sting
as he falls deep into slumber,
a disconcerting discomfort
which he does not quite identify.

Three days later, the *Oafus* is back
in his element, and sits in a stupor
in stop at a traffic light.
His eyelid is purpled and swollen,
the ophthalmic Medicated Goo
has blurred his left vision,
and the pink pill antihistamine
has left him loopy. Before him,

multi-colored giant jelly beans
pour through their allotted shunts
like corpuscles through vessels,
and all the lights in his sight are as red
as colonies of *serratia marcescens*
growing in domes out of petri-dish agar.

"The Blood of Christ," he mutters,
light-headed and light-blind.
He mourns the loss of his mechanical
eye shields, as self-diagnosis
and self-medication have been proven
insufficient as prophylactics of pain.
He thus sits and suffers, and wonders
what he might have done differently
to have dodged his present dilemma.

On The Nature Of Madness

Insanity is a bad dream from
which you cannot awaken.

It can begin as a buzzing fly taken
by the lips of a waiting Venus,
weighty grains in the folds of oysters,
an artichoke whose spiny leaves
re-furl to hide a tender heart,
or a Glass Onion that can neither be peeled
nor peered through.

It will grow into a consumption,
a well-armed emerging Minerva
that can't be extracted by
Vulcan's broadest hammers or
the sharpest skills and scalpels
of a surgeon.

You can talk no one; your
thoughts and words are enemies.
Your friends turn their back on you,
your family will shun you;
your father will not look at you long
enough for him to read
your reaction to the ultimate
question which he must pose.

Doubt pervades, fear ensues;
your feet are lead,
there is iron in your lungs,

shouts in your head,
the shining pearl of sickness fast
affixed to your gray tissues,
and long will you be in labor with
the tiny internal albatross
of mind.

A Seed Is Planted

It is said that water oaks
spend half their lives growing
and the other half dying,
but their lives span
just a half-century;

but live oaks can survive
for hundreds of years;
upon reaching full maturity,
they spread and sprawl luxuriously;
their branches dipping to the ground,
they provide shade and shelter
for houses, schools, and squares,
canopies for Southern streets,
playground sets for children,
and homes for hundreds of chirpers.

Regal, revered, and regaled,
they are deeply embedded
in our heritage and culture,
in our art, music, and literature,
and are ubiquitous fixtures
in our native landscapes,
both urban and country:
they are the true Queen Mothers
of all things green and growing,

but unlike their figurative roots,
their nutrient systems are shallow
and run parallel to the ground;

thus, they are often bowled over
by a storm or a hurricane,
and leave behind a wide crater
when turned on their sides.

I will plant this year a live oak
out back behind my house,
knowing well that like me,
I will never see it
reach its full potential.

Four Stages of Goldfish Pond

They come to the edge
to nibble fish food from
extended fingers.
The neighbor calico finds
easy pickings, licks his
paws on each catch.

Invading frogs over-
populate the waters,
tadpoles thick as crickets;
while fish die of
nervous fright.

A summer proliferation
of pond lotus chokes
off the sun, oxygen
deprivation resulting;
dead fish, bloated,
float to the top.

The plastic liner breaks,
the water drains out,
the pond a depression,
a receptacle of permanence
for trash plants
in cracked pots.

Twenty Years Too Late (Again)

The Arlington is all run-down,
the Majestic is crumbling,
the Park does not deserve a stand,
and Happy Hollow is sad.

The architecture on the Row
is a living stone testament to ghosts
of gangsters, gamers,
and old ball players.

Mom and Pop have been moved out;
the chains have taken over Central,
nothing is left but boutiques, galleries,
and motels and restaurants that die hard,
so visitors are stragglers.

The Quapaw and The Buckstaff
are still okay, they say;
we tour The Fordyce,
now a national park museum.
Spaces between stalls are small,
the equipment calcified and antiquated;
we drift whispering through a ward
reminiscent of the hydrotherapy
and electro-shock
of the Cuckoo's Nest.

My life companion,
feigning the skeptic,
demands to see the source,

and is not satisfied until
we survey the open cascade
and steaming pool below.

I see little evidence of inbreeding here,
but most of the women have hair loss.
I ponder the cause of that effect;
the locals drink the waters by the gallon,
available for free to all that gather
at the public filling places;
so, who is to know?

Pedestrian Crossing

His ears are his eyes,
his white cane an antenna,
his nose an instrument
of navigation, and he uses
every square inch of his skin
for sensation.

Cars in front and left are idling,
and he smells his destination,
the burger shop across four lanes.
Cars on his right roar by
as he feels their wake on his arm.
With certainty of right-of-way,
he steps off the curb, following
his cane, and crosses two lanes gingerly,
feels for the concrete divider,
deftly side-stepping the same,
then hurries across the last two lanes
with the hope that any right turners
will see him.

Up on the sidewalk,
his cane is a depth finder,
and its tip in the turf tells him
of a slight earthen elevation.
Two steps upward puts him
into the parking lot, and
with several steps forward,
he finds the building.

He turns left on the raised walkway,
and ambles along the wall of glass,
his right hand waist high and sliding,
reaching for a door handle
that he cannot find.
Then his cane tip hits brick,
and he realizes that he has gone
the wrong way, and is backwards
next to the drive-through lane.
He reverses and retraces his path,
left hand now coursing the glass,
and finds again the building's corner.
He then makes another left,
going toward the front doors,
and disappears.

A Dry Run

I huff soberly on what's left
of last night's mighty spliff,
my lines loose and not stiffening
as I wait in anticipation
of something good to come.

The sun is well up,
now at quarter staff,
but its light is diffused
by a thatch of grey clouds
that cast a pale shadow
on the brown brackish waters
of the western inlet.

Three little chicken legs
are my only wards, lying
forlorn at the ends
of strings, but the east
wind blowing blows me
no good, and as is the case
with my three kids, now grown,
I wonder what it is
that's not working.

I have been late
for most of my life,
but today I broke pattern,
woke early, even earlier, I suppose,
than those tasty crustaceans
that won't take the bait,

but the minnows hit and strip it
to bare bones.

Both sun and I need
to make some new breakthroughs.

Ditch This Summer

The bridge on Louray Street ,
its span barely the length
of a winged Thunderbird,
bears no name.

Beneath it, a rivulet flows
sleepily in pools, chunks
lining its sides and bottom
a betrayal of any claim
of naturality.

Stones not of this soil
form the bed of this body,
their mounds dark islands,
smooth and rounded.

A rusted drainage pipe
runs between green yards above,
a chance for little boys
to test their balance.

The neighboring cypress
casts long shadows down
to the slim bank below,
its boscoyos budding antlers,
breathing air for growth.
Twin dragonflies chase each other
up the run.

Wait. One of the rocks

is a terrapin snapper,
perhaps of late expired.
Toss a pebble down,
splash right next to it,
'ploosh!' It moves slightly,
well alive still.

Shell in the sunlight,
feet in the drink,
this turtle has it made.
It shifts to revert
to its preferred position
of repose.

Flip down to brown still water
a used-up unfiltered butt,
soon to degrade to naught,
and cast far from the turtle.

Haiku Easter Sunday

is a whippoorwill
an onomatopoeia?
bird linguist needed

green herbs in the box
Rosemary is still dead brown
Spring sprang without her

red brick in the ground
my Easter egg hunt first prize
dig it up for keeps

Winnie snatches crumbs
a bit of chocolate egg
where did my mind go?

don't forget the theme
Christ has died Christ is risen
will Christ come again?

another day trip
off to the old fishing pier
what will we find there?

Pre-Destination

If you want to comprehend
the concept of The Road,
you must take a long night ride
on an old federal highway
through a vast country-side;
interstates do not provide
the same frame of mind or feel,
there's far too many cars out there,
and it's just too big a deal.

When you hit the hill country
that starts outside of town,
you'll dispel your slight night jitters
by the right use of your headers,
as you don't want to out-drive your lights.
Put your brights on when you might,
but cast them down and away
when a fellow night traveler
comes the other way.
Watch the crossings and turnarounds;
that's where troopers hunker down
like white birds of prey awaiting
to catch the fly-by-nights,
speeding and accelerating,
that come into their sights.

Let your music set your mood,
tunes that move and groove, but soothe;
it needn't be Americain
or even a Canadien,

whatever are your preferred genres,
put some on and sense the wonder;
whether Bob Wills, Black Keys, Bach, or The Beatles,
open up the window some,
and smell the sweetness of pine needles.

You by-pass cities
and cross through counties,
traversing villages and towns
where your highway, now a by-way
runs through what still are downtowns,
boarded-up buildings, mostly shut down,
as all the business went away
when the Interstate went the other way;
but when you hit each city limits,
brake and obey the speed limits,
as lurks out there a lone deputy,
somewhat frustrated, truly bored,
waiting beside the Dairy Queen,
or behind the Ford billboard,
and he'll chase you down
and maybe take you in,
for the slightest of scowls
or the silliest grin.

Eventually, you start to see
that you're part of this humanity,
your place here certain and necessary,
like sleeping town-folk lying in bed
in their darkened, quiet homes,
or the lonely, wizened denizens
of the local nursing homes,
like inmates in the county prisons,
whose razor wires and hot bright lights

cast a far pall in the night.

You'll be at certain times distracted
by detours, junctions, and promises of action,
but your destined route lies straight ahead;
all the road signs point that way,
and you will have to function well
when tomorrow is today,
so keep your treads on the right track,
and do not go astray.

Your butt starts to ache, and your eyes turn red,
so you better pack some gum,
smoke them if you have them,
or use the console as a drum;
and try to stay up on your toes:
The Road can be deadly,
as everybody knows,
when you're driving late at night
and your eyelids start to close.

Ultimately, it gets in your head
what Brother Gregg meant when he said
that The Road goes on forever,
but you will reach your destination,
so you'll stop and you'll get off;
but even after you have settled
in your hotel double bed,
your wheels will still be spinning,
and you won't sleep like The Dead.

The Insane Game

It is bit like the Roman Senate;
all the contestants wear togas
and mill about the floor,
muttering threats and insults
to each other.

The live studio audience
is a Greek chorus,
shouting commentary,
encouragement,
and criticism.

I am still a rookie,
but have started a new school;
I raise high my voice
and swear like a plebian;
I am wildly popular,
and my tenure seems assured.

The elders are startled and scared;
a plot is afoot already
to do me in.

The Clay Model

Although technically not filled with clay,
the clay model is a new device
in the administration of criminal justice.

It looks somewhat like a toothpaste tube,
only much shorter and wider,
and is filled with a doughy synthetic substance
that is totally D.N.A.-sensitive.

A single tear is obtained from the offender,
oft-time by exposure to sliced onions,
then is dropped into a syringe of saline solution,
and after a short waiting period,
the mix is injected into the tube
through the top opening,
then the tube is re-capped.

After an over-night incubation,
the tube is sliced across the bottom,
and gently squeezed on both sides
to reveal the white clay inside.
Tiny figures then begin to form and move,
complete as to act, actors, and scene,
re-creating the crime in question
in every exquisite detail.
The scene will repeat itself
until the tube is crimped shut.

The hope is that the offender
by watching himself commit crime,

will feel some sense of remorse,
but the statistics must yet be compiled
and analyzed by an array of experts.

Work continues in the labs
on making the clay viable longer,
and a version in full color
is still in the planning stages.

Regrets

I bludgeon myself
every once and again
with clock-hammer
brick-bats, lost time
that has been;

I view past decisions
with doubt in redoubt
on a high promontory
where I lie alone,
and the fool on this hill
has no eyes
and no clothes;

I refuse to see clearly
what's been laid before me,
and I cloister myself
in a series of No's;

but with time at low tide,
my regrets can't subside;
so I dry my red eyes,
and then thumb my long nose.

Oak Ridge Summer '68

My parents tried to pack
two bottles of bourbon
between the linens stacked
in the hitched U-haul.
They both broke, probably
against each other; the sheets
stained, and the pillowcases tore.

All the labs and offices,
as well as the lakes and creeks,
had official alphabet names;
we swam and fished in a park lake
called Y-2; they later found
unhealthy levels of radioactivity
deep in its bottom shelves.
No wonder we never caught
even a single fish.

The apartments were red brick
four-plexes around a cul-de-sac.
Their most interesting feature
was basements I'd never known,
cold, clammy, and frightening,
unless the dryers were on.

The evenings were so long,
we had daylight past 9:00 p.m.
After supper, everyone played
volleyball in the front yard,
even my mom.

One of the lab scientists
was doing research on fireflies;
we collected them by the jar.
They made great night lights,
and we cashed them in
to buy comics, Cokes, and candy bars.

I played a lot of whiffle ball
with a nice colored kid
from Jonesboro, Arkansas.
We didn't have a bat, so
it was just balls and strikes,
each of us umpiring for the other.

The 24-hour virus came by
for a week-long visit.
Mom fed us chicken noodle soup.
I threw up so hard
the noodles flew out my nose.

After five rounds of Putt-Putt,
my buddies and I
had doughnuts and coffee
at the local Krispy Kreme.
Mom had a near-fit;
I was too young to drink coffee.
I do not drink coffee
to this very day.

We named all the lab dogs
after Tolkien characters.
Frodeaux was the spare,
and he suffered no testing.
We brought him home in August.
He was the best pet ever,
and I miss him still.

The Quiet Unrequited

The quiet unrequited live
in homes without walls,
and everyone can see
whatever they do.

They creep down halls,
too timid to knock
on closed doors.

The quiet unrequited are
lied about.

They go walking
at midnight,
look in any window,
search for silhouettes
on the shade.

The quiet unrequited keep
a respectful distance.

They write sad poems
that nobody reads,
sing sad songs
that nobody hears.

The quiet unrequited,
at a failure for words
and unable to act,
fail themselves.

At Land's End

At the edge of a choppy sea,
I stand on a small spit of beach,
and before the ocean's roar,
good thoughts seem out of reach.

I cannot swim or surf;
I haven't the right attire.
I cannot walk the shore;
my feet in sand are mired.

Unlike the tiny pipers,
the wavelets I will not flee;
my feet have been wet before,
I need now to wet my beak.

I stand a silent statue,
a lighthouse darkened, gone,
my mouth has watered sour,
and I need a catharsis to come.

Inside The Passage

A space, whether large
or small, remains a space,
and largely defines a place.

The inner berth is a small
and windowless place,
but there is enough space
for two beds, a closet,
and a full bath. Its pitch
is much less than that
of the balcony suites
out by the bow,
as is its price.

The immense banquet hall,
boasting its Stilton, lox,
au jus, and tasty pastries,
is accessed by an entry
so slender as to be clogged
by two old codgers with walkers.

The salmon of Ketchikan
flee the vast sea to climb up
narrow river ladders,
and join their siblings
gathered in one small space,
the place where they are born,
return to spawn, and pass on.

The small capital of Juneau

has no roads in or out,
no airport, and no tall spires,
but the bars are full,
and the natives are lively.

The glaciers are huge,
cold, and ice blue,
and impress on you
the idiocy of trying
to hike them or fly atop
in a helicopter.

The mountains that surround,
green from sky to ground,
provide a scenic backdrop
for nature's chicanery,
rolling otters, an awkward walrus,
the crash of a splashing stray whale;

but, in time, your eyes start to strain,
the vistas, so clean and pristine,
never end, like a strange dream,
and you see through the panorama
of evergreen paradise that you are trapped,
a small animal on an ornate treadmill,
afloat in an elaborate palace
of purgatory.

Upon embarkation
at the end of your vacation,
the long road to Anchorage
provides more of the same,
and you wonder whether or not
everything has changed;

then, rounding a sharp bend,
you glimpse the golden scallop
of a new Shell service station;
your breathing comes more easily,
you begin to feel normal again.

Fruit Of The Womb

With one grandiose sweep of his hand,
the Younger knocks over his gold goblet
of red wine, and its contents splash
onto the lap of the Older like
a crashing wave hitting sand.

Immediately uncomfortable,
and a little disgruntled,
the Older is first tempted to temper,
but as juices seep through his robe
and moisten his undergarments,
a familiar sensation arises below,
so he flies down from Olympus
in search of a two-legged sow
in whom his seeds he'll sow.

Their product is a hybrid,
half grape and half man,
who can still be seen today
in certain underwear ads.

The Younger, still high above,
cackles at the mischief he has caused.

Turistas Chingadas

In the *Mitte* of Berlin,
within the grandeur of antiquity
and the splendour of modernity,
lies the Holocaust Memorial,
a Flanders' Field of tomb-
shaped slabs, unmarked
and anonymous, equal in size,
which appear by the hundreds
in a symmetric block, equi-
distant from each other,
along a slope that seems to rise.

All the visitors, save three,
both domestic and foreign,
have lost completely
any sense of decorum;
they leap from slap to slab (*verboten*),
chase each other through the spaces,
use the pathways for a maze;
most laugh and shout,
and take selfies on cell phones,
as if they have no notion
of what this place is about.

I want to walk up the slope,
toward the higher ground,
but I quickly discover
the effect is illusion;
the pathways sink deeper
and the tomb-slabs rise high,

and within a few yards
I can scarcely see the sky,
so the message of the artist
cannot be mistaken.

I pose for one head shot,
a draped forearm
on the top of one plinth,
my head cupped by one hand
atop a propped elbow,
somber and composed
for the cover photo
of a future tome.

Another Child Of God

Her doe eyes rapt,
the tiny celestial angel,
no bigger than three,
stands silently in awe
of the chocolate fountain,
its rich waterfall
unending; brown ribbons
descend in concentric circles;
this is the newest
wonder of her world.

She cannot see the pool below,
the pretzels, strawberries,
and marshmallows waiting,
the sticks used for dipping,
she is transfixed on movement,
and knows without reckoning
that this muddy river
will taste so sweet.

A tall man walks
in front of her,
and the spell is broken;
she glances down
at the floor, then turns
to look for her mother.

After The Flooding

Once the waters recede,
all of the foliage
up to the flood line
is covered in mud
and silt which is soon
wind-cooled and sun-dried;
what remains is a brown
powder on leaves, branches,
and berries, ghoulish
in its shroud-like appearance,
as if whole sections of forest
were cast in plaster;

but the next line of showers
will wash all this away,
and the woodlands will become
homogenous again.

This is how
the alluvial earth
replenishes itself.

The Rhubarb

It started in the bottom of the third
on a balk that wasn't, or maybe it was;
Manny's foot was more than a foot
in front of the bump when he whirled
and faked a snap throw to first.
The home plate umpire came out
onto the infield and signaled
the runner down to second;
any move toward first that emphatic,
he said, required a throw regardless
of contact with the rubber.

Manny tried to plead his case,
and Barry came out of the dugout to argue;
Mike in left and Corey in center added
their snide comments, and the bench buzzed.
Barry came back grumbling, and play ensued,
but Mike and Corey were pouring it on,
and two pitches later, the base ump turned
to face them, and threatened their ejection
if they didn't shut up and quick,
but he didn't call time out first,
and what would have been a called
third strike went as a No Pitch,
then everybody started to bitch.

Manny was in a rage, and Barry went back out
to again engage the plate ump. Raucous calls
rolled across the field and out of the dugout,
from which Frankie emerged uninvited.

Barry tried to tell everyone to calm down,
but Manny was beside himself, and when
the plate ump told him to zip it or else,
Manny screamed, "Or else what?"
and he was immediately tossed.

Manny's reaction was to hurl the ball
as hard as he could toward the plate;
it bounced in the dirt, and was blocked
by Nick, our catcher, but the plate ump
turned and called out to the park manager
to call the police, as he had just been assaulted
with a baseball. Frankie continued agitating,
and he got tossed, too, as he had no business
being on the field. The plate ump then asked Barry
for Manny's full name, but Barry wouldn't give it up,
so he got tossed as well, and left the field fully disgusted;
the rest of us shaking our heads in amazement at the sight
of forty year olds, both in white and in blue,
acting like a bunch of fourth-graders.

Manny was seething in the dugout
when we told him to pack his ball bag and leave quickly;
he said, no, he wanted to talk to the cops.
I assured him he most certainly did not,
and that he might well be taken in if he remained.
He finally left the dugout, but parked himself in defiance
on a small knoll for several minutes before departing.
Barry tried to manage from the bleachers, but the plate ump told him
if he couldn't watch quietly, he'd have to leave.
Barry beseeched the park manager, who shrugged,
then he went out to the parking lot to call in
his complaint to the tournament directors
and the association's top-ranking officers.

While he was gone, we shuffled the line-up
and finally got to play with Barry's pull-tab
plastic roster board, which nearly made him bananas
when he saw us doing it. He screamed at us to stop,
and used his wife and Ed to go to and from
his bleacher post with directions.

We tried to use the rhubarb for motivation,
but it was already way too late;
the train was off the tracks,
and we crashed and burned to a crisp;
we were ten-runned after seven innings,
but idiocy was the true winner that night.

The cops actually came to the park, it seems;
they accosted Frankie, who told them that he too
was a cop (true), and that he didn't know Manny's
last name or at what hotel he was staying.
They were satisfied with that, and left
to pursue more important matters,
probably coffee with Krispy Kreme.

Tikaremu

Outside in the rain,
Monkey Man stands,
underneath the overhang,
lit nubs in both hands.

He sees that the seedling
he had once spared
is now a mature red oak
that rises high against gray skies.

One of his offspring
will soon be married
into a Greek-American clan,
the parents Greek,
the children American
but still very much Greek,
and so is in the process
of converting.

He is trying to learn
some small phrases in Greek,
so as to be friendly,
but like all monkeys,
he is easily confused
between Hello and Goodbye,
Please and Thank You.

He thus devises a plan,
in typical Monkey fashion,
for the creation of a word,

non-real and nonsensical,
to use as a fall-back
in case he is tongue-tied,
and he puffs on both nubs
as he seeks the right term.

It comes to him soon,
and he lets out a laugh;
the fake word is perfect,
and will draw mixed reactions.
He helplessly giggles,
his pants getting wet,
then he sees his child eyeing him
through the French doors.

Pyrites

Batten down loose loopholes lingering,
and draw tight the dotted line.
Enough tacking and yawing.
We contract compactly,
the wind taken out our sails.
We strike our respective flags.
Tie up the loose ends,
hold the rope and drop anchor;
may there be surety in our bond.
Break out fine rum and cigars;
together we carve seals in wax.
We have made ourselves an island,
one conjoined body incorporate
without corporeality.
May nothing cause us to drift apart,
not even the currents of currency.

Venus In Capture

One raised hand pulls gently back
her still-wet flowing heather locks;
a lowered hand holds lightly
a silk sash newly loosened.

Her eyes closed, her face serene,
one cheek turned to the wind,
the ocean air lifts hair and hem;
above the subterfuge of waves,
her dainty foot points downward
toward seas from whence she came.

Scallop shells and snails surround her,
bedded, like her, in gray plaster;
now she endures a new capture,
tiny winged stinging soldiers,
earthworks all around her;

and so her basin remains empty,
untouched by the human enemy,
and barren, here is where she'll stay,
walled above a shaded walkway.

In Search Of Religion

Before my initial convocation,
using the fledgling prophet's website,
I was able to procure a living fish
from one on-line devotee
and transfer it to the MySpace of another.

At the meeting that followed,
he bade us to dance in place,
but in conjunction with each other.
All was going well until
an apparent infidel took the stage
and punched him in his face.

I chased him across the hollow
and beseeched him for an explanation.
He pretended not to hear me.

At my second sacred revival,
we were given loaves of pumpernickel,
and told to pass them among ourselves.
My wife told me not to trade loaves
with Kay-La from Malaysia;
she was infected with The Disease,
and was seeking the prophet for a cure.
I put my bread down on the altar,
and endured some angry glares
from zealous followers.

In the adjoining bazaar,
I ran into my dead friend.

He was selling the prophet's teachings
in the form of cartoons as clever
and coherent as those in magazines.
He tried fervently to tell me
how these works were especially relevant
to one in my situation,
but remembering how he and his whole family
were all schizophrenics and bat-shit crazy,
I was strictly a no-sell.

At my third and final summit,
the prophet cast his line across the waters,
but the fish he lured had its own mind,
found legs and crawled out from the river
to trod the hostile desert sands,
and the crowd amassed grew quickly uneasy.

Body And Soul

The body is the building
that houses the soul, but
houses too can have a soul,
and in old houses, the souls
will speak in the tongues
of wood.

The soul of an old house
is deep between its walls,
in its attics, its crawl spaces,
the sills of doors and windows.
Many a structure of durable roof
and sturdy pillars hide within
the sickness of rot, mildew, and
mold which coat the soul
in slow black suffocation,
and the bones of the body suffer
the torment of rodents and insects
that burrow and chew.

The body parts must thus be restored,
rehabilitated, repaired, or ripped
out and replaced, or the house
will be lost, as will its soul,
as exteriors often wither from within.

Wellness is to look after your body,
but look also into your body
for the wellness of your soul.

In The Off Season

The beach at Old Orchard is empty now,
and the town is mostly shut down.
Steel beams of the grandstand and roller coaster echo
the happy laughs of children long since gone.
Some remains of a clambake sit silent in wake
as a half moon looks askance on a vacant bay.
Only the trees reflect the color that was,
the sun slides behind the hills that surround,
and the traveler leaves a lone
set of footprints in the sand.

In Last Night's Strange T.V. Movie

The anti-hero was a professor
of psychology whose extra-marital
affairs, both straight and gay,
and rampant recreational drug use
were driving his poor wife
to distraction.

The wife was an employee
of a major corporation
whose offices were a jungle
atrium six stories in height,
with platforms for work spaces
and automated vines hanging all around
for transport between floors.

Her boss was a bellicose
Machiavelli, whose booming
voice rattled the atrium's windows
and made the natives of the jungle
run for cover and hide behind
their desks.

His wife was an embittered shrew,
childless, and without enough to do,
so she spent most of her time
poking her pointy nose
into the business of others.

The leading couple's child
was confused to the point of autism,

avoided contact and speaking with people,
and was deep into therapy
by age eight.

His therapist was sympathetic,
an adjunct teacher at the college,
and thus an underling to the anti-hero.
He knew the child's greatest obstacle
was the instability of his parents,
but felt powerless to say so,
as he needed the extra income
to support his aging mother.

They all lived in a small college town
in the Midwest, attended the same church,
and were members of the same social
beneficent organization.

At that year's annual banquet,
the boss' wife, as event director,
snubbed the professor and his wife
by placing them at the table farthest
from the podium and not in keeping
with their positions as officers.

The professor's wife, fed up,
demanded of her husband
that he redeem their status
by confronting her boss' wife
and obtaining new seating
appropriate to their station.

The crowd went quiet in anticipation
as the professor approached the stage.

He went directly to the shrew,
interrupting her welcoming speech,
and whispered in her ear.
She hissed at him, and pushed him aside,
so he picked up a bowl of ambrosia
and dumped its contents on her head.

He then threw the punch bowl into the crowd,
followed by the roast beef and gravy,
and announced to all he was leaving
to live with his gay lover and
his straight lover in a cabin in Colorado,
where he would write the next great novel,
and quickly, as long-held festering
resentments boiled over and exploded,
and fist-fights broke out and ensued.

Les Miles, playing himself as
featured speaker, smoothed things over
with patent hand gestures and a turf roller,
explaining that the solution was
uniforms: everyone, he said,
needed his or her own uniform,
and that the uniforms needed
to be uniform, save the numbers.

In the aftermath, the wife,
now unemployed, was consoled
by the therapist, who confessed
his long-standing admiration
and attraction. His prospects were good,
he said, as the college had offered
him her husband's vacated chair,
and the son, sitting quietly
in the corner, cracked a smile
for the first time in ages.

Midnight Rider

Under a June blue moon,
he shinnies down the drainpipe
to the patio below, and creeps
down the gravel driveway,
his pace quickening on reaching
the tree-lined avenue. Soon
he is thumbing on the city streets,
hitching rides to the railroad crossing
where Ben Hur Road meets
Nicholson Drive.

There, he hides in the tall weeds,
and waits for the old ten-twenty,
its coming forewarned by the long
low whistle moans rising on approach.
The freight slows for the last passage
on its way out of town, and he spies
an open boxcar coming into range.
He jumps up and runs, sprinting aside
the tracks, then lunges for the door handle,
knowing not to miss. Grip secured,
he deftly lifts his legs up,
and rolls into the freight car,
and so the show is on.

He must be back by daybreak,
but his destination is New Orleans,
as the Brothers are packing the Warehouse,
likely for the last time, their star
ascending, and Blue Sky ahead.

Nothing to do now but wait, and smoke

his Marlboro Reds. He gropes
the clutch of sweaty dollars
in the pocket of his jeans, insurance
against his inability to sneak through
the grimy back-alley bathroom window
he leaves unlocked each time.

As he rides and dozes, he visualizes
Duane and Dickey re-tuning
their twin sun-burst Les Pauls,
relaxing backstage in preparing for
an extended late second set.
He leans back against the metal wall
and dreams of Sweet Melissa, already
In Memory of Elizabeth Reed.

Lefty

Only one white mouse
in the great lab cage
quit the nicotine spigot,
sniffed but once at the cocanoid,
hated the taste of alcohol,
and avoided like plague the opioid,
instead preferring the cannabinoid
and the mellow glow he so enjoyed.

They all called him Lefty,
for the cannabis spigot
was the one to the far left,
also in joking reference to
the left-handed cigarettes
that humans like to roll
and smoke.

All of the cool mice
hung around sipping nicotine,
and more than occasionally cocaine,
but these made Lefty feel jumpy;
and on his one try of coke
he thought he'd had a heart attack.
The sad mice drank ever-clear
or dabbled in smack,
but booze led to hangovers,
and H left Lefty's bones wracked;

so he sucked on the pot spigot
alone, without company,

and while sometimes it seemed
he was perpetually hungry,
his food pellets always
were taken as tasty;

and on the off days,
when the spigots were closed,
he would watch the other mice
run nervous in nicotine fits,
shiver with quivers and shakes,
undergo horrible withdrawals,
or suffer the delirium tremens,
but Lefty would stay
as calm as he pleased,
knowing that in another day
he would savor more extract
of his beloved sweet leaf.

In Passing

A block from the cross-roads
at the heart of Port Barre,
the rest stop is a small plot,
green grass on a single lot
shaded by pecans,
nothing but a picnic bench
and a blue port-a-potty;
still, it invites.

Just past the outskirts
of what was old Alex,
a cemetery is crowded,
and the close-laid graves
look like concrete braces
stacked in a train yard.
This might be the destiny
of all wide-open spaces,
if we last long enough,
until Judgment Day comes.

At the graveyard for cars,
the corpses line up
in straight rows of twos,
doors and hoods open
in surrender to Fate,
while one hundred white egrets
watch from tall cypresses
next to a borrow pit
that once was a pond.

The cloud up ahead
is a pig on the run,
chasing temptation,
an end of all mystery.

Her Father's Daughter

The middle-aged Asian man waits
near the entrance to the new casino
for his squat female companion,
his wife or perhaps a sister,
in totter and lagging behind.
As she approaches, it is seen
that she is in fact his daughter,
short, fat, and Mongoloid,
her bespectacled eyes in deep squint,
the tip of her tongue stuck out
as if to sniff the rarefied air
of opulence.

Once inside, he guides her
to the blazing dragon slots
that promise all good fortune;
there they play together side-by-side,
her round face aglow
in the bright red light
of a perfect playground
seldom seen
through the eyes of a child.

Room 107

He is semi-reclined in a wheelchair,
eyes closed, limbs and chest bare,
his surgical scar
an angry red ravine.

You touch his shoulder lightly,
call his name softly;
his eyes open and try to focus.
You tell him who you are;
he murmurs your name,
grasps both your hands,
tries to gather his strength.
His arms reach up,
drape around your shoulders;
he brings you to him
for a last embrace,
buries his face in your neck;
you hear his soft sobs.

You tell him everything is all right,
everything is taken care of,
that he needn't worry.
His arms relax and release,
fall to his sides;
his eyes close slowly
as he recedes into
his opiate dreams.

Japanese Women In Black And White

Eldest daughter
hiding in the hall closet
bids me to lift her dress
but I cannot do it
her fabric is too stiff

Auntie in the viewing room
watches television from the sofa
I slide my hand across her shoulder
she puts her hand on my leg

Grandmother is incensed
and tries to burn the house down
I give her my matches

Mama-San is anguished
by the gathered water
and looks at me in askance
we will have to move again

One From The Cajun Navy

A brown burlap bag floats
down an overflown stream;
swirling crazily in current,
in a hurry to destruction
or deposit in the Gulf,
just another piece of flotsam
in the wake of the flood.

Three youths in a bateau,
not of this city or state,
pull alongside in curiosity,
try to haul the bag aboard;
it is surprisingly heavy.

Hoisted over the bow,
the bag hits boat bottom;
the loud thump of dead weight;
the bag rolls over to reveal
an old brown woman inside.

She is not breathing.
and has likely died,
but the boys try to revive her,
and through no small miracle,
she survives and is still alive,
so they give her a ride
all the way back to safety;
she needs more care still
than they can give her,
and they have more rescues
to provide.

It matters not that she is brown,
nor that they are white;
it matters not that they are bigots
and wave the Confederate flag
from the bumper of their truck;
they are there to do good works,
far from home and far from alone,
and all lives matter to them
in this dire time and tide.

Wool-O'-The-Wisp

The unmown spring lawn,
a micro-cosmos of meadow,
is a green pond awash
in quick-sprouting grasses
and inedible herbage;
dandelions, buttercups,
and clumps of clover abound;
tiny white flowers atop long stems
hover above in observance;
a lone thistle in thorny crown
stands taller than all, bristling
in its dare to be chopped
and trimmed for its tasty stalk,
at the risk of the pricking of fingers.

The soft south breeze puts all in sway,
drawing a gaze with the seduction
of simplicity, transfixing the viewer
in a temporary rapture as deep
and mesmerizing as the four-
hour fixation of the junkie
with his foot while on a nod.

The events of the day
pull the viewer away,
and as he mounts his ride,
he thinks it a shame, in a way,
to plow it all down,
but he knows what must be done,
over and over,
until winter comes.

American Dream: The Movie

The premise of the film
is somewhat unusual, in that
the same recurring dream script
is performed and recorded three times,
with each version shot separately,
but all three are intended
to be identical in all particulars.

The object lesson is that despite
the most meticulous attention to detail,
none of the repeated episodes
looks or feels exactly the same;
no fly can stay on the same wall forever,
shadows inevitably grow longer,
and voices reciting the same lines
contain subtle changes in nuance
that are easily and readily discerned.

By the time of the third repetition,
the viewer realizes that he or she
is the dreamer.

Still Waiting

Drops are sucked through sand screens
in the diffident March of dotage;
two elms of Desire lean together,
top-heavy with gravitas,
in wait of eventual Fall.
Their barks are coarser than ever,
roots exposed and weakening,
and they have slowly hardened,
too dry now for new growth,
but they whisper to each other
in hope of regeneration
from the Spring arising.

To My Octogenarian

In the aftermath of my late call,
I anticipate the hoedown,
I contemplate your eightieth,
and I peer obliquely back to days
of thin black business suits under lab coats,
only one car and waiting outside,
pursuits of spotted lepidopterae,
chantarelles and condo steaks,
and matrices of cotton bolls.

(the phenom baller and his stodgy father
had to use your phone;
the cow barn palace afforded them
no such luxury)

I do not want to look like you,
thus the facial hair,
but look like you I must:
it's all there, squatted legs
on a boiling pot cauldron.

(an attendant of the wedding
observed us together
and said we were a cluster shock)

I took much from you:
a fascination with nature,
an appreciation of history,
a celebration of good life,
the eyebrow of annoyance,

a disaffection with religion,
and alcohol;

but much did I miss:
the ability to be clear,
decide rightly,
and abide;
being governed only
by common sense.
(I still dally often
and sometimes wallow in despair).

So as you cross life's penultimate bridge,
know that I too am making
a crossing of sorts.

I see the irony in your retirement,
but it does not affect you;
I sense the futility of my gift,
but it is pretty and may please you;
and while I celebrate your day,
I will not pray to God for you,
as you would not want me to;

and I say to you
what some day I long to hear:
live long, old man.

A Private Viewing

Over the last few weeks,
in the last full hour before dawn,
my wife has watched from our picture window
five fox kits that frolic each morning
on the lawn that fronts our home.

They run and jump, she says,
and chase each other into and out of
a clutch of cat-tails near the street,
but when she appears for her daily stroll,
they run away through a neighbor's fence,
afraid, to a den unknown.

I have seen their mother
trot across the driveway
when I get home in the evening,
and creep across our back yard late at night,
but it is not my destiny to see them,
as I am not an early riser by norm.

C.B. says they are not a threat
to the nearby dogs and cats,
but I call bull-shit on that; besides,
some of our neighbors have chickens.
I tell my wife to post a notice
on the Association website,
and to call Wildlife & Fisheries.
She won't make the call, though;
despite my assurances
of safe capture and relocation,

she says that if she calls,
they will be killed.

I think she just enjoys having
her own private Nature channel,
one without commercial interruptions,
where her mind's eye and her memory
are her personal cameras of choice.

Impressions Pre-Parade From A Country Mardi Gras

The teen-agers stroll quickly
up and down the parade route,
trying to be nonchalant,
but their excitement shows.

The old folks sit in folding chairs
along the parade route,
trying to look complacent,
but their weariness is as plain
as the lines on their faces.

The breezes wafting
off the oxbow lake
feel good on the back
of your neck.

Catfish, frog legs, chicken, shrimp,
onions rings and funnel cakes;
everywhere, the smell
of good food frying
permeates, overwhelming
the burger stands
and barbecue pits.

The women of south Louisiana
are more handsome than those
of most other places,
and more vivacious, too.

The local bars and bistros

have opened their doors
to the streets, and hawkers ply
the passers-by with Mimosas,
Bloody Marys, and, of course,
cold beers in big cups.

The biker dudes and biker chicks
are overweight and all over fifty,
and the hair under their bandanas
is mostly gray.

Hunters' khakis rival traditional
gaudy purples, greens, and golds
as the revelers' fabrics of choice
in garb and accoutrements.

The kids are giddy with throws
from the last parade: beads,
toys, noise-makers, and snacks,
the rubber hand grenade a hot item
this year. A tow-head boy
brandishes his tiny plastic sword
with true bravado.

Cops and members of the Lions Club
drive cars, cycles, and four-runners
up and down the parade route
on missions of certain importance.
One fat deputy can steer a Hummer
and eat a bowl of jambalaya with only
two hands.

The crowds are thinner, more congenial,
and less pressing than their big-city

counterparts. You will be able
to go easily to and from the curb,
and you can pick up fallen doubloons
without fear of stomped fingers.

The native ethnic gumbo
has new ingredients stirred in,
and mixed-race couples are no longer
stared at in curiosity or disdain.

The girls here ripen early
and must grow up very quickly,
since their men remain boys
forever.

Everyone knows everyone,
save you, the urban visitors,
but before you leave,
you will meet somebody
you've known for years
from the city.

Ho Hum

Sitting in an airport,
waiting for a plane,
I am struck by
the people emerging,
not by their diversity,
but by their
commonality:
we are all passengers
on the same plane,
and each of us
has his own
flight to take;

and as I examine closely
each passing person,
I glimpse in each one
the little glimmer
of a soul.

This brings to me
tranquility,
and my fear
of death subsides
for a while.

Parrains

The white frame house with louvered shutters
has long since disappeared from the bend
in the river road at old Convent,
but the thin sliver of farm land,
reaching back to the forty arpent mark,
sans the double rows of pecan trees
that once graced it in majesty,
is still there, as is the side street
marker that bears my family's name.

Parrain is the French word for godfather,
and this was the country estate home
of my parrain, after whom I am named.
My father's uncle, he left Nouvelle Orleans
as a young man to settle and raise a son
in the old plantation lands upriver.
He was an educator, a notary public,
and a community leader, a founder
of the famous Catholic retreat at Manresa.
He spoke with a slight French accent,
and told me wonderful made-up stories
about characters such as Johnny Watermelonseed
and Peter Balloonjuice. I cherish the memories
of our trips to St. James Parish to visit him
and his tiny, wiry wife Odette.

I too am a parrain, as one of my good friends
asked me a long time ago to stand as godfather
to his only child, a son. It seems like yesterday
that we gathered in the St. Louis Cathedral

of our French Quarter for the christening.
My godson is not of my blood, nor of my name,
but has always called me Parrain, and seems
genuinely fond of me. I have tried well
to be a good parrain; we went together
to football games at the great stadium
of our state university, and we share
a love of good music and guitar playing,
but he has grown up, and we have grown apart,
and I have often wished I had been more to him.

We buried his father some months ago,
and we shared in presenting the eulogy.
I was surprised by his humor and composure
in the face of his great calamity, and I reminded
him how much his father loved him.
I now redouble my efforts as parrain,
as I am the only father he has left,
and this is my sworn sacred duty.

At Mallard's Bluff

Out by the vast rookery,
through a wooded passage,
we enter the cypress cathedral,
where there are no pews or ushers;
knobby parishioners, young and old,
gather in familial clusters.

The canopy is forest green,
the floor brown carpet,
standards unhewn columns,
windows open air;
the flooded lot
holds but two bateaus.

Here, we are the movement,
as there are no pastors,
but we sense
a higher presence
up above.

The Hope Of America

A young teen strides suburban streets,
his cheeks in flush and teeth bared,
already in a hurry to get there.
Along the lawns of his neighbors
he scurries, struggling to hold onto
an old weed whacker with one hand
and a used hedge trimmer with the other.
A new extension cord thrown
over his narrow shoulder,
he is hustling well into August
to make some hard-earned
summer bread, some to save,
some to spend.

Body Parts

My head is a periscope;
it pivots and peers,
but does not see much.
The lens is smeared.

My fingers are like sausages
that have been cooked badly;
they're burnt around the edges,
but near-raw in the middle.

My legs are tree trunks,
gnarly and knotty,
and just about
as immobile.

My feet are blocks of concrete.
I'm not going anywhere.

My stomach is an angry bear
that lives in a cave
by itself.

I have no chest.

A Short Dive From The Low Board

That summer, the sun beat down on us
like it was the Devil himself;
we scampered for shade
into the thickest woods,
and drank a lot of hot water
from the garden hose.

The neighborhood pool was our savior,
our clear crystal blue oasis.
As soon as our summer membership began,
Mom started taking us to the pool
nearly every morning in June,
and we would often return again
with Dad late in the day.

On one sunny sojourn,
the Lackie twins and I
had the diving board
to ourselves; we performed
cannonballs and can openers,
jack-knives and swan dives
to our collective hearts' content;
then we noticed that the lifeguard
had left temporarily his nearby post,
so we quickly concocted a plan.

We decided that the thing to do
was to all jump off the board
in rapid succession, taking
care not to land on each other,

so we prepared for the leap,
John in front, me in the middle,
and Jim taking up the rear.

John ran off the board,
and as I started to follow him,
I saw the lifeguard emerge
from the snack shop,
looking directly at me,
his face contorted with anger,
and about to shout, blow
his whistle, or both.
Busted, I stopped at mid-
board, and tried to turn around,
but in so doing, I ran into Jim,
lost my balance, and fell off
to the side like a poul-doux
being shot from the sky.

Time slowed to a crawl
as I rapidly descended;
I had no time to extend
my arms, and I landed
face-first on the concrete.
Stunned and numb, I drew
myself to my knees, checked
my face for blood, and found none.
My vision was awash in waves
as I staggered to my feet
and wobbled over to my mother
in her pool-side recliner.
She comforted me as I cried,
for once not scolding me
for doing a bad thing.

Jim got off the board gingerly,
and went to the spot where I fell.
He found there a small piece
of chipped tooth, picked it up,
and brought it to my mom.
She wrapped it up in a damp napkin,
summoned my little sister,
and took us home.

Dr. Lorio gave her concussion instructions,
and held me out of two baseball games.
The dentist said there was no way
to re-attach the chip, but that a cap
on the tooth was a viable alternative.
I declined, and to this day, one
can still see the chip in my upper incisor,
a permanent reminder of my
short dive from the low board.

Of Dreams

The Noble Dane did miss the mark:
"To sleep, perchance to dream,"
for whether 'tis in light or dark,
in sleep, we always dream.

Some dreams are lost in a gray blur,
not waking up in time,
some dreams occur and then recur,
their meanings deep, sublime.

Some dreams I have are dear and sweet,
others are murd'rous rage,
some dreams I send to you replete
across this printed page.

Someday, I'll have a dream from which
I will not be awakened,
an end to life without a hitch,
if I'm a lucky one.

The Final Cut

It starts with an evening phone call,
a sales pitch for time shares in Cancun.
A booming voice offers him five days' stay
in a representative condominium, free,
including air fare and all expenses,
meals and airport shuttle included,
if he will attend while there a morning seminar
entitled "Save Your Soul Through Self-Control,"
and a short sales presentation following.

His usual skepticism at first prevails,
but the lure of a winter vacation lingers;
he worries not about succumbing to a purchase,
as his will power is strong and proven.
He talks to his wife about the proposal,
and she is enthused, especially upon hearing
of daily organized activities for the kids.
After two hours of discussion,
he calls up the toll-free number
and accepts the offer, and after
the usual telephonic clerical details,
he hears a recorded message from Booming Voice,
thanking him and promising him
that he will not be sorry.

The flight down is smooth sailing,
the kids content and playing in their seats,
and the resort is all that was advertised,
their condo spacious and well-furnished.
As the formal activities will begin the next day,

they spend the afternoon around the pool,
sipping drinks and watching the kids ride the slides.
His wife says she feels as if someone is watching her,
and sure enough, from across the broad expanse of water,
he spots a slender blonde man peering at them intently,
who gives him a sly wink on detection before disappearing.

The next morning, he attends the first two-hour seminar,
quickly bored by the stale power-point presentation
and the ceaseless recitations of stock platitudes.
He notices the blond man from the pool sitting
not far from him among the dozen other attendees.
The blond man, younger than he, arises from his chair,
gives him another surreptitious wink, and leaves,
not to be seen for the duration of the lecture,
cut mercifully short due to equipment malfunction.

His early arrival back to the condo startles his wife,
who is sweating and somewhat unsettled.
She has just returned, she reports, from the work-out room,
and has had a near disaster with a faulty Nautilus.
He suggests they report the problem to the management,
but she demurs and quickly changes the subject.
They spend the day together on the adult-only beach.

The next day, ten minutes into the second lecture,
the same scene plays out: the stand-up, the wink,
this time with an irritating smirk, and the departure
of the blond man without a word from anyone.
He is angered that apparently the other is beyond
the requirement of attendance, and determines
to leave himself, and to follow this odd fellow.

He stalks the blond across the compound,

who makes a circuitous route to their condo.
A light tap on the door, and his wife answers,
still in her gown. They kiss and embrace briefly
before she shuts the door behind them.

His blood boils. He leaves the resort,
crossing the street to a neighboring pawn shop.
He buys a beat-up revolver and a small box
of bullets, loading the gun as he grits his teeth.
He stations himself in a bush near the condo,
and waits. Soon the door opens, and the blond appears,
blowing a farewell kiss of cuckoldry back into the love nest.
He bursts from the bush, his vision blurring,
and fires a wild shot into the chest of the paramour.
Blood splatters everywhere as the blond stares
at him with fatal comprehension, then falls
forward to the pavement, motionless, his limbs
splayed awkwardly in the crumpled posture of death.
Blood pools on the sidewalk as his wife emerges
and screams. He stands stupefied, now fully aware
of what he has done, and in petrification
at his prospects of life in a Mexican prison.

Music begins blaring from the courtyard loudspeakers,
and people come pouring out from everywhere,
but to his shock, they are laughing, cheering, and pointing.
A camera crew appears, as does a mariachi band,
and resort staffers pop mini-champagne explosives.
A florid man attached to the Booming Voice rushes forward,
giving him effusive thanks of amused appreciation.
The blond man rises and extends a limp hand,
and he realizes he has been duped and played for a fool,
and that everyone was in on the ruse, even the pawn broker
that had sold him the gun and the bullet blanks.

Booming Voice congratulates him; he is the new poster child
for loss of self-control and the consequences which follow.
His reward, upon accepting his role and cooperating fully
in its complete and documented video exploitation,
is a free time-share for life in the resort's ritziest suite,
one week per summer, with all the amenities.

After the contracts are signed and tomorrow's monologues arranged,
he and his wife take a late lunch at the pool-side Tiki bar.
His wife is consoling and apologetic, but there is a look
of triumph on her face she cannot conceal completely.
He cuts into some complimentary prime rib as she relates
all the details of the scheme, hatched weeks before
the initial telephone solicitation. She pats his hand sympathetically,
but he feels a small flicker of rage which slowly grows.
She asks him if didn't he think the whole affair was at least
a little bit funny, and he says he guesses it was, chewing glumly.
He then picks up his steak knife and stabs it into his wife's face.

Last Night

"There is no crime of which I do not deem myself capable"
Goethe

I hurt my daughter deeply
because she would not answer me,
and upset my wife terribly
in the hideous process.

My rage begat a rampage,
and I savaged our hotel,
punching holes in walls,
destroying furniture and fixtures,
and shooting the lights out.

I went on a murder spree,
machine-gunning indiscriminately
through closed doors and windows,
slaughtering scores and wounding
hundreds of others.

I took hostage a young country music star,
but her pretty face was too recognizable,
so I let her slip away.

I became the most wanted quickly,
the manhunt after me held
law enforcement officers
from every level.

I was apprehended, tried summarily

without benefit of a jury,
convicted, and sentenced to die
without benefit of appeal.

I was executed, liquidated
in a most peculiar way,
and was sent to hell by God
for all eternity.

All within a few hours,
then it was all over.

In Any World Of Hurt

One day as a child,
I burst into tears;
I told my mother
I would never be happy.

It had nothing to do
with my station in life;
my childhood and upbringing
were normal in every way.

No, what I think it was
was a sudden realization,
a loss of naiveté,
an initial understanding:
life is filled with trials,
tribulations, and travails;
no one can be happy
all the time; and only
the lucky among us
will live long enough
to age, sicken, and die;

but what I have discovered
in the years that have intervened,
is that in nearly every life,
there are moments of happiness
that must be recognized and
savored, collected, and cherished.

The feeling may arise from

ordinary instances: the patter
of rain on a tin roof, cumulus
clouds moving slowly like a fleet
of freighters across a blue sky, or
the company of family or friends.

 It may be something as simple
as a little Chinese baby girl that
puts her head on her shoulder
and gives you her sweety eyes,
then waves her hands to and fro,
babbling in animated baby-speak
about things that you can't understand.

Look for these golden nuggets,
and put them in your shirt pocket;
keep them close to your heart.
They will see you through
in any world of hurt.

In Case You Missed the Engagement Party

The Grand Ballroom at The Canal Westin
held nearly four hundred people.

The guests were an eclectic mix
of Asians, Greeks, and Americans.

The Vietnamese and Chinese great-nieces and nephews
played two tunes in a string/drum ensemble.

The food was good American fare,
steak, potatoes, haricot verts, Caesar salad.

The band was flown all the way in
from the Greek island of Chios.

The presiding Orthodox priest came over
from the groom's local Greek church.

The families adorned their new members
with gifts of fine jewelry and watches.

Vows were taken and rings were exchanged
for a wedding a year away.

The dancing began after dinner,
and went on past two a.m.

The Asian-American girl and her Greek fiance´
were goddess and god on the dance floor.

The *bouzouki* man played clean and quick,
the deep clarinet blasts otherworldly.

The couple was showered with small bills,
all swept up as tips for the band.

The proud mother of the groom
baked Greek cookies and imported others.

Everyone danced the Greek two-step;
the circle went 'round and 'round.

The groom's father brought his home-made *souma*,
sweet, potent, and so very tasty.

The elders went home fairly early,
excepting the Greeks, of course.

The groom, his brother, and his dad
swayed long and low, arms spread wide.

Jordan almonds in white silk bags
were given as parting gifts.

The father of the bride danced two times,
and finally managed a smile.

A Tiny Stone

A tear in the eye
will not dry, nor
evaporate; it will
find its own way
onto a man's face,
and only then be
brushed aside;

for tears do not form
within the eye proper,
but rather within the heart.

The tear duct is a tiny stone
that must be rolled away.

What Is Left

Fig trees produce ripened fruit
past the Indian summer
and well into September
or October.

Harvest time for sugar cane
and most citrus varieties
is after the first cold snaps.

A sun that's soon to set,
glowing gold in a sky of red,
casts a scenic splendor
like no other heavenly body.

The D-string of a guitar,
wound brass thread-bare
and near to popping,
makes an exquisite hum
not otherwise heard.

Flounder run out of the marshes
when the weather turns cold,
and return for Valentine's Day.
Look for moving water.

Many featured films
craft their sunset scenes
by recording sunrises
to play in reverse.

Leaf, Snake, And Butterfly

I must not be
like a leaf
on a tree,
blown by the winds,
turning brown,
dying and falling
to rest on the ground.

I must not be
like a snake
in the tree,
shedding its skin
as each spring begins,
each time becoming
its same self
again.

No, I must be
like a butterfly;
leave my cocoon
on the bark of a tree,
spread my wings to dry,
reach a state
of final grace,
and fly
for the rest
of my time.

The Trick To Elevation

The trick to elevating yourself
is the pre-flight preparations:
you must empty yourself
of all heaviness and distraction
by means particularly suited,
a blue Miles immersion,
some driveway Tai Chi,
or the cat poems of Sandburg,
to reach a state of levity.

You need the blessing
of fair and mild weather;
go into your front yard,
make a stand on level ground,
take a few deep breaths,
and allow your mind to become
completely unfocused.

Put your hands at your hips,
palms down. Push earthward firmly
but gently the air below them
over and over again.
Do not let doubt or worry
weigh upon you. Constancy
in your hand movements,
with practice and exertion,
will bring you equilibrium until
you slowly rise from the ground.

Your initial excitement and amazement

may make you lose equanimity. If so,
you will start sinking. Synchronize
your efforts, and find your stroke,
and you will learn how to stay afloat,
get more lift, steer, and maneuver.

When you've risen to tree-top heights,
beware of electric wires overhanging.
Go carefully around them with due caution,
and once you are clear, catch
the prevailing wind, and go!

John Lambremont, Sr. is a poet and writer from Baton Rouge, Louisiana, U.S.A. John's poems have been published internationally in many reviews and anthologies, including Pacific Review, Clarion, The Minetta Review, Raleigh Review, Sugar House Review, and Words & Images, and he has been nominated for The Pushcart Prize. John's most recent full-length poetry volume is "The Moment Of Capture," (Lit Fest Press 2017). His other poetry volumes include "Dispelling The Indigo Dream," (Local Gems Poetry Press 2013), and his chapbook is "What It Means To Be A Man (And Other Poems Of Life And Death)," (Finishing Line Press 2014). John's full-length poetry collection "The Book Of Acrostics" will be published later in 2018 by Pure Slush Books.

Pski's Porch Publishing was formed July 2012, to make books for people who like people who like books. We hope we have some small successes. **www.pskisporch.com**.

Pski's Porch

323 East Avenue
Lockport, NY 14094
www.pskisporch.com